FAVORITE ILLUSTRATIONS

Children's Classics

IN COUNTED CROSS-STITCH

Ginnie Thompson

DOVER PUBLICATIONS, INC., NEW YORK

Preface

This is a book of counted cross-stitch designs, and something more—for the designs are adaptations of the works of three of the world's best-loved illustrators: Sir John Tenniel, W. W. Denslow and Kate Greenaway. Although their styles are distinct from one another and their personalities dissimilar, Tenniel, Denslow and Greenaway had two attributes in common. One, they drew a kind of truth that is instantly recognizable and, two, they shared a delight in the universal republic of childhood.

To the child in each of us that recognizes the truth and remembers the joy, the spirit of fun and delight remains. With that delight, choose the colors for the Greenaway frocks and hats, high-waisted trousers and frilled collars as painstakingly as Kate did. Use corals, salmon, terracotta, moss green, honey brown, French blue, dove gray, shell pink, buttercup yellow—whatever is your delight. Make Tenniel's Cheshire Cat disappear and reappear across a child's placemat. Put Alice looking up at the cat on a napkin or bib, so that the child may look first at one cat and then the other. Put a Tin Woodman, a Scarecrow and a Cowardly Lion on a hanging of pockets. Put bills or report cards in the pockets, and let the Tin Woodman, the Scarecrow and the Cowardly Lion remind you that having a heart, a brain and courage are the requirements needed to face a life full of humbugs, false-colored glasses, tornadoes and witches.

Cross-stitch a little of the delight that Tenniel, Greenaway and Denslow had in all children. Cross-stitch for the special child you love and for the child that is still within all of us.

Published in Canada by General Publishing Company, Ltd., 30 Lesmill Road, Don Mills, Toronto, Ontario.

Published in the United Kingdom by Constable and Company, Ltd., 10 Orange Street, London WC2H 7EG.

Favorite Illustrations from Children's Classics in Counted Cross-Stitch is a new work, first published by Dover Publications, Inc., in 1976.

International Standard Book Number: 0-486-23394-4
Library of Congress Catalog Card Number: 76-18404

Manufactured in the United States of America
Dover Publications, Inc.
180 Varick Street
New York, N.Y. 10014

Introduction to Cross-Stitch

Counted cross-stitch is very simple. The basic ingredients are a small, blunt needle and a fabric that is woven so evenly it appears to be formed in regular blocks or squares. Push the threaded

DIAGRAM 1

needle up through a hole in the fabric and cross over the thread intersection (or square) diagonally, left to right *(diagram 1)*. This is half the stitch. Now cross back, right to left, making an **X**. That is all there is to it! But beware—this simple process is very addictive. For the sake of it women neglect their husbands, homes, children, jobs, churches, community affairs and their own good looks. (There is no telling what male cross-stitchers neglect, but it does seem unfair that they win so many of the top awards.)

Counted cross-stitch is an ancient skill that has been practiced and perfected with slight variations in technique all over the world. Here in America and in Denmark, too (where cross-stitch is a fine art), the bottom stitches traditionally slant left to right and the top stitches right to left. In England, however, the stitches slant in the opposite directions—oh well, the English drive on the "wrong" side of the road, too! It really makes no difference which technique you adopt *as long as you are consistent* throughout your piece of work.

In America an embroidery hoop is used, and the work is done with the stab stitch, in which one comes up through a hole on one journey and then goes down through the next hole in a separate journey. In Denmark, however, cross-stitchers use a continuous sewing-stitch motion, and the work is done without a hoop. Where our diagrams appear to show sewing stitch, it is merely for visual clarity.

SUPPLIES AND EQUIPMENT

1. A small blunt tapestry needle, #24 or #26.

2. Evenweave fabric. This can be linen, cotton, wool or a blend that includes miracle fabrics. The three most popular fabrics are:

COTTON AIDA (Pronounced "ada," "ida" or "eye-ee-dah," like the opera). This is made 14 threads per inch, 11 threads per inch, 8 threads per inch, and so forth. Fourteen, being the prettiest, is preferred.

EVENWEAVE LINEN. This also comes in a variety of threads per inch. Working on evenweave linen involves a slightly different technique, which is explained on page v. Thirty-count linen will give a stitch approximately the same size as 14-count aida.

HARDANGER CLOTH. This has 22 threads per inch and is available in cotton or linen.

When purchasing or cutting fabric for a project always allow a pleasing margin around all four sides of the design *plus at least* 1½ inches all around for finishing and mounting. Don't skimp—better to waste some fabric than your work.

3. Embroidery thread. This can be six-strand mercerized cotton floss (DMC, Coats and Clark, Lily, Anchor, etc.), crewel wool, Danish Flower Thread, silken and metal threads or perle cotton. DMC embroidery thread has been used to color-code the patterns in this book. For 14-count aida and 30-count linen, divide six-strand cotton floss and work with only two strands. For more texture, use more thread; for a flatter look, use less thread. Crewel wool is pretty on an even-weave wool fabric, and some embroiderers even use wool on cotton fabric. Danish Flower Thread is a thicker thread with a matt finish, one strand equalling two of cotton floss.

4. Embroidery hoop. Use a plastic or wooden 4″, 5″ or 6″ round or oval hoop with a screw type tension adjuster.

5. A pair of sharp embroidery scissors are absolutely essential.

6. The last essential is a good strong light. Optional aids are a "stitch-finder," a metal sheet with magnetic strips that slips under the design to mark one's place, and an "around-the-neck" magnifying glass.

WORKING FROM CHARTED DESIGNS

Don't confuse counted cross-stitch with the cross-stitch embroidery you may have done as a child, where large X's were stamped on a piece of cloth. In counted cross-stitch the embroiderer works from a graphed or charted design and, by coming up through one hole and working diagonally over the thread down into the opposite hole, makes a perfectly even stitch. This is actually much easier to do and much less frustrating than trying to make a perfect stitch by working over a stamped design. Most counted cross-stitch designs, like those in this book, are plotted on grids of ten squares to the inch, as this makes them very easy to read. Whatever the size of the grid, each square on the chart represents a cross-stitch on the fabric.

While some cross-stitch charts are printed in color, most charts are printed in black and white, using different symbols to denote colors. This system allows for unlimited shadings and the use of many, many colors. Since embroidery floss is in-expensive, enormous color choice is one of the joys of counted cross-stitch.

Bear in mind that the finished piece of embroidery will not be the same size as the charted design unless you happen to be working on fabric that has the same number of threads to the inch as the chart has squares to the inch. To determine how large a finished design will be, divide the number of stitches in the design by the thread-count of the fabric. For example, if a design that is 112 stitches wide and 140 stitches deep is worked on 14-count aida, divide 112 by 14 to get 8, and 140 by 14 to get 10; so the worked design will measure 8″ x 10″. The same design worked on 22-count fabric would measure approximately 5″ x 6½″.

HOW TO BEGIN

Prepare the fabric by whipping, hemming, or zigzagging on the sewing machine to prevent ravelling at the edges. Next, locate the exact center of the design you have chosen, so that you can then center the design on the piece of fabric. Most of the designs in the book have an arrow at the top and along one side; follow the indicated rows to where they intersect; this is the center stitch. Next, find the center of the fabric by folding it in half both vertically and horizontally. The center stitch of the design should fall where the creases in the fabric meet.

It's usually not very convenient to begin work with the center stitch itself. As a rule it's better to start at the top of a design, working horizontal rows of a single color, left to right. This technique permits you to go from an unoccupied space to an occupied space (from an empty hole to a filled one), which makes ruffling the floss less likely. To find out where the top of the design should be placed, count squares up from the center of the design, and then count off the corresponding number of holes up from the center of the fabric.

Next, place the section of the fabric to be worked taughtly in the hoop; the tighter the better, for tension makes it easier to push the needle through the holes without piercing the fabric. As you work, use the screw adjuster to tighten as necessary. Keep the screw at the top and out of your way. (Right-handed people usually keep it in the "10 o'clock" position; lefties in the "2 o'clock" spot.)

The length of the thread should be from the bend of the elbow to the fingertips, plus a little bit, say about 18 inches. The "spit and push" technique is used for threading the needle. When beginning, fasten thread with a waste knot by

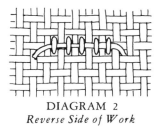

DIAGRAM 2
Reverse Side of Work

holding a bit of thread on the underside of the work and anchoring it with the first few stitches *(diagram 2)*. Do all the stitches in the same color

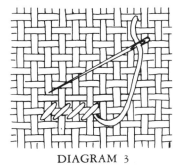

DIAGRAM 3

in the same row, working left to right and slanting from bottom left to upper right *(diagram 3)*. Then cross back, completing the X's *(diagram 4)*. Some

DIAGRAM 4

cross-stitchers prefer to cross each stitch as they come to it; this is fine, but be sure the slant is always in the correct direction. Of course, isolated

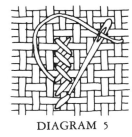

DIAGRAM 5

stitches must be crossed as you work them. Vertical stitches are crossed as shown in diagram 5. Holes

are used more than once; all stitches "hold hands" unless a space is indicated. The work is always held upright, never turned as for some needlepoint stitches.

When carrying a color from one area to another, wiggle your needle under existing stitches on the underside. Do not carry a color across an open expanse of fabric for more than a few stitches as the thread will be visible from the front. Remember, in counted cross-stitch you do not work the background, only the fun (design) part.

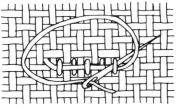

DIAGRAM 6
Reverse Side of Work

To end a color, weave in and out of the underside of stitches, perhaps making a scallop stitch or two for extra security *(diagram 6)*. Whenever

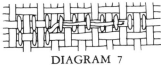

DIAGRAM 7
Reverse Side of Work

possible end in the direction in which you are traveling, jumping up a row, if necessary *(diagram 7)*. This prevents holes caused by work being pulled in two directions. Do not make knots; knots make bumps. Cut off the ends of the threads; do not leave any tails because they'll show through when the work is mounted.

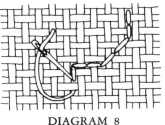

DIAGRAM 8

The only other stitch used in counted cross-stitch is the backstitch. This is worked from hole to hole and may be vertical, horizontal or slanted *(diagram 8)*.

LINEN TECHNIQUE

Working on linen requires a slightly different technique. Evenweave linen is remarkably regular, but there are always some thin threads and some that are nubbier or fatter than others. To even these out and to make a stitch that is easy to see, the cross-stitch is worked over two threads each

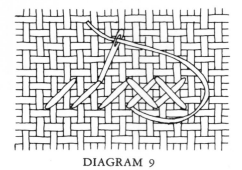

DIAGRAM 9

way. The "square" you are covering is thus 4 threads (diagram 9). The first few stitches on linen are sometimes difficult, but one quickly begins "to see in two's." After the third stitch, a pattern is established, and should you inadvertently cross over three threads instead of four, the difference in slant will make it immediately apparent that you have erred.

Linen evenweave fabric should be worked with the selvage at the sides, not at the top and bottom.

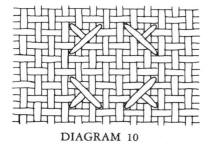

DIAGRAM 10

Because you go over more threads, linen affords more variations in stitches. A half stitch can slant in either direction and is uncrossed. A three-fourths stitch is shown in diagram 10. Diagram 11 shows backstitch on linen.

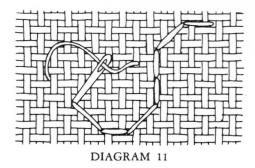

DIAGRAM 11

FINISHING

After you have completed your embroidery, wash it in cool or lukewarm water with a mild soap. Rinse well. Do not wring. Roll in a towel to remove excess moisture. Immediately iron on a padded surface with the embroidery face down. Be sure the embroidery is completely dry before attempting to mount.

To mount as a picture, center the embroidery over a pure white, rag-content mat board. Turn margins over to the back evenly. Lace the margins with button thread, top to bottom, side to side. The fabric should be tight and even, with a little tension. Never use glue for mounting. Counted cross-stitch on cotton or linen may be framed under glass. Wool needs to breathe and should not be framed under glass unless breathing space is left.

Cross-stitch supplies and fabrics are available in an ever-increasing number of needlework shops. However, if you are unable to find a source in your area, write to:

Cross-Stitch, Dept. D
P. O. Box 825
Pawleys Island, S.C. 29585.

Many cross-stitchers join the Counted Thread Society of America, 3305 S. Newport Street, Denver, Colorado 80223, which sends out several informative and enjoyable newsletters each year. The annual membership fee is $3.

To Tommy, Joe, Peggy
for our mutual love of
children's books and
counted cross-stitch

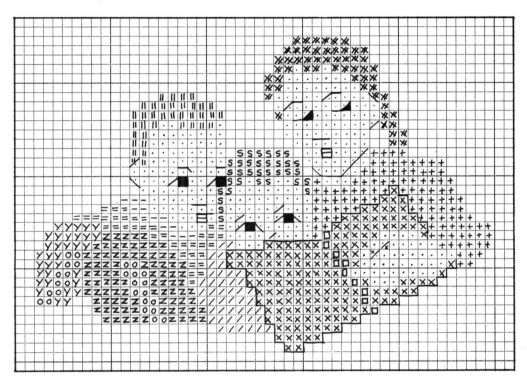

COLOR CODE:

DMC #

Ⅲ	437	light brown
🗶	433	dark brown
S	435	medium brown
◢ ◼	801	very dark brown; backstitch eyes
⊡	818	flesh pink
🆅	760	pink; backstitch face details
⊞	642	gray beige
🗶	817	red
⬚	816	dark red
⊿	712	cream
Ⴜ	839	dark beige
O	842	light beige
🆈	840	beige
⊟	827	blue
⊟		white

The White Rabbit as Court Herald

Size: 67 x 84; centers as marked

DMC #

COLOR CODE:

☒	642	beige; backstitch head, legs, whiskers
☐	776	light pink
◪ ■	956	deep pink
⊡	957	pink
⊙	335	rose; backstitch ruff
☒	309	dark rose
ℕ	3072	very light gray; backstitch banner fringe
⊞	415	light gray; backstitch tabard
◪	318	dark gray
☒		silver metallic
⊟		ecru
Ⅲ	644	beige; backstitch end of scroll
▲	597	turquoise; backstitch cord to seal

Alice and the Bottle Marked "Drink Me"

Size: 49 x 83; centers as marked

DMC #

COLOR CODE:

◿	420	brown; do eyes as shown, backstitch brow
☑	422	light brown
⊡	818	light flesh pink
⊡	776	dark flesh pink
▣	760	pink; backstitch nose, chin line
☒	813	blue
☑	334	medium blue
◎		white
⬚	647	gray; backstitch tag on bottle
�	3328	rose
▮	825	dark blue
	928	gray; backstitch stockings

5

The White Rabbit with a Watch

Size: 38 x 73; centers as marked

COLOR CODE:

DMC #

◪ 956 bright pink
◼ 776 pink
⊡ 818 pale pink
☒ 640 beige; backstitch head, ears, whiskers, legs
▣ 3046 mustard
◉ 825 blue; backstitch umbrella handle
◎ 783 topaz
⊟ 780 dark topaz; backstitch jacket, watch chain
✓ 725 saffron gold
☑ 355 rust; backstitch vest details

NOTE: To achieve plaid effect, work the jacket in cross-stitch in topaz (◎), then backstitch over the topaz stitches with dark topaz (⊟).

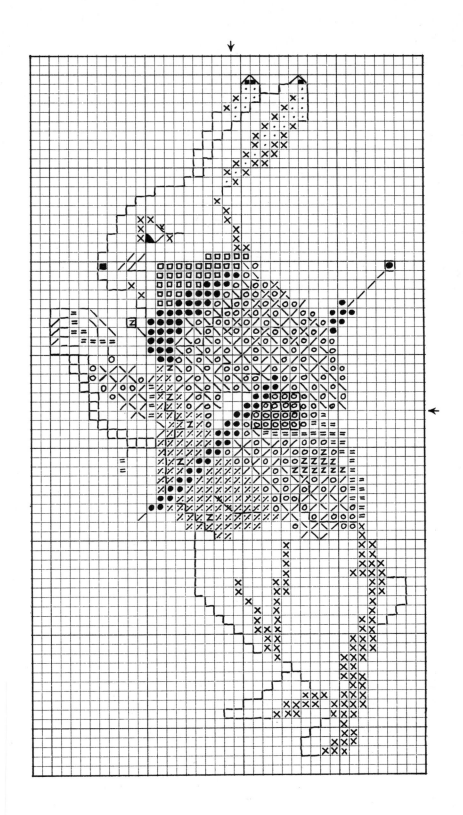

Alice and the Pig Baby

Size: 40 x 66; centers as marked

DMC #

COLOR CODE:

	DMC #	
◥	310	black; backstitch pig's mouth
⊟	3046	yellow
Ⓢ	3045	honey brown; backstitch brows
⊡	818	flesh pink
◼	433	brown; backstitch eyes, shoe straps
☒	813	blue
▨	825	dark blue; backstitch collar, pinafore
⊙	761	salmon
	956	bright pink; backstitch bonnet, Alice's mouth, nose
⊞	347	rust; backstitch pig's nose
	928	gray; backstitch stockings
▨	760	dark salmon; backstitch details on pig

Alice and the Cheshire Cat

Size and centers not given (depends on placement)

DMC #

COLOR CODE:

Ⓢ	471	spring green
⊞	839	gray brown; backstitch tree
⊠	433	brown
⊻	353	salmon
⊙	905	dark bright green
⊡	907	bright green
⊚	434	light gold brown
⊟	436	very light gold brown
⊠	938	very dark brown; backstitch details on cat
▣		white
⊘	731	olive green; do as half stitch
Ⓒ	597	aqua; backstitch skirt
Ⓥ	612	tan
⊠	3046	yellow brown
⊙	991	dark green; backstitch stockings
⊡	818	flesh pink
⊘	726	yellow
Ⓟ	598	light aqua

NOTE: To make cat "disappear," work eyes, ears, nose, grin and chin in full cross-stitches *(see detail)*. Work tree trunk and leaves in full cross-stitches. Work body of the cat in half stitches to blend with the half stitches of the shadowy leaves (⊘).

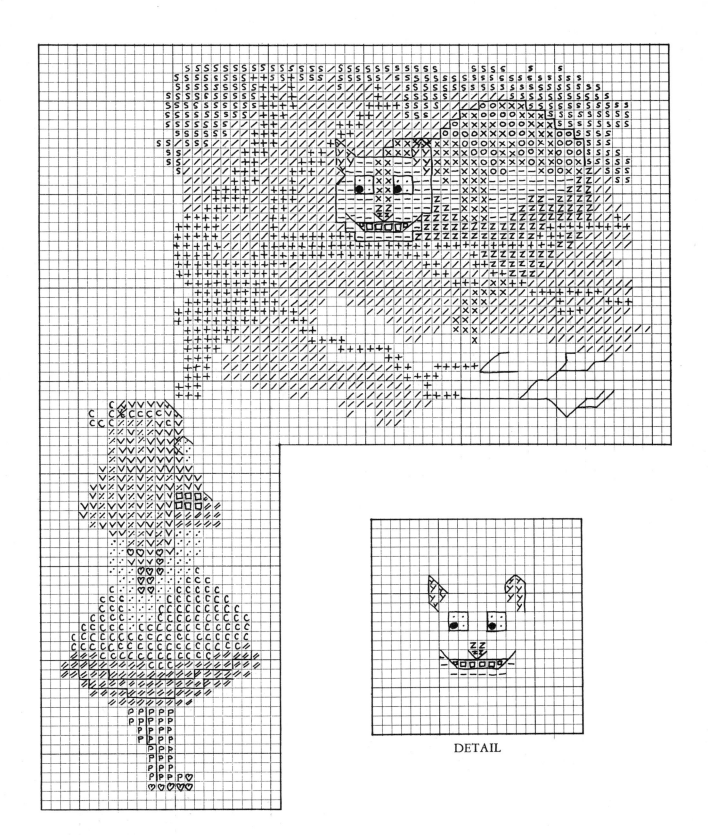

DETAIL

Kate Greenaway Girl on a Stool

Size: 30 x 72; centers as marked

COLOR CODE:

DMC #

⊟	353	light coral
⊠	352	coral
⊠	807	blue
▲	433	brown; backstitch tendrils of hair
⊡	225	flesh pink
⊞	646	gray; backstitch shawl
⊠	648	light gray
⊡	598	blue
⊠	842	tan
⊻	840	dark tan
⊠	702	bright green
⊘	704	light bright green
■	645	dark gray
	760	pink; backstitch neck

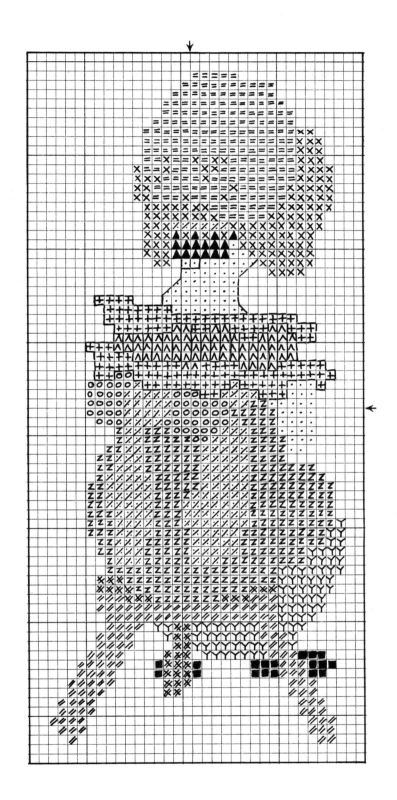

13

Bubble Pipe

Size: 43 x 58; centers as marked

COLOR CODE:

DMC #

☒	3328	rose; backstitch shirt, collar
⊟	814	dark red; backstitch pants
⊙	761	light rose
⑤	743	yellow
⊡	225	flesh pink
■	433	brown; backstitch eyes
⋀ ⊟	760	medium rose, backstitch nose
⊟	842	light beige brown
ℕ	840	medium beige brown; backstitch stockings
⊻	647	gray; backstitch pipestem
ℤ	598	blue; backstitch bubble
	436	very light gold brown; backstitch hair

Big Sister

Size: 22 x 90; centers as marked

DMC #

COLOR CODE:

	DMC #	
⑤	640	gray brown
▣	519	turquoise
⊡	818	flesh pink
◼	938	dark brown
☒	3013	light green
▨	422	light tan
▨	3045	tan
◎	827	blue; backstitch baby's dress
▨	963	pink
⊞	3012	green
	760	pink; backstitch mouth, nose

Strawberries

Size: 34 x 26; centers as marked

DMC #

COLOR CODE:

	DMC #	
⊞	907	light green
☑	3347	medium green
☒	304	red

Children Embracing

Size: 29 x 54; centers as marked

DMC #

COLOR CODE:

	DMC #	
◉	336	dark blue
⊡	963	flesh pink
▣	334	medium blue
◭	813	light blue
⊟	208	violet
♡	335	rose
⬆	957	light rose
⊞	760	very light red
�	841	beige brown; backstitch legs
⑤	938	dark brown
▨	3013	light green
⊟	644	medium ecru
☒	818	pink
◈	433	medium brown
☒	3046	mustard
Ⓝ	3047	light mustard
▨	223	faded pink
◪	435	medium umber
⊞	760	pink; backstitch face, arms

16

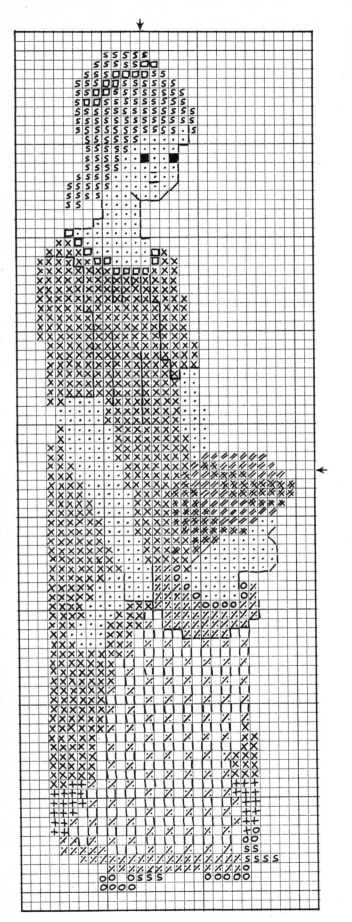
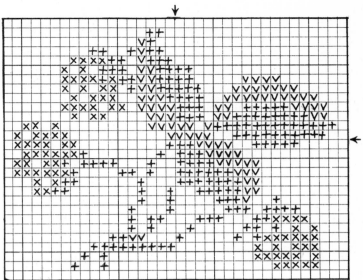
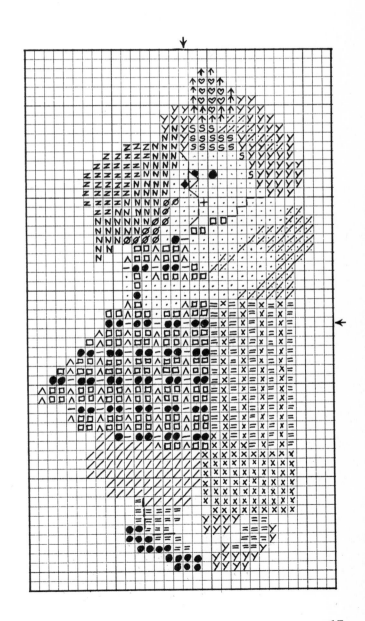

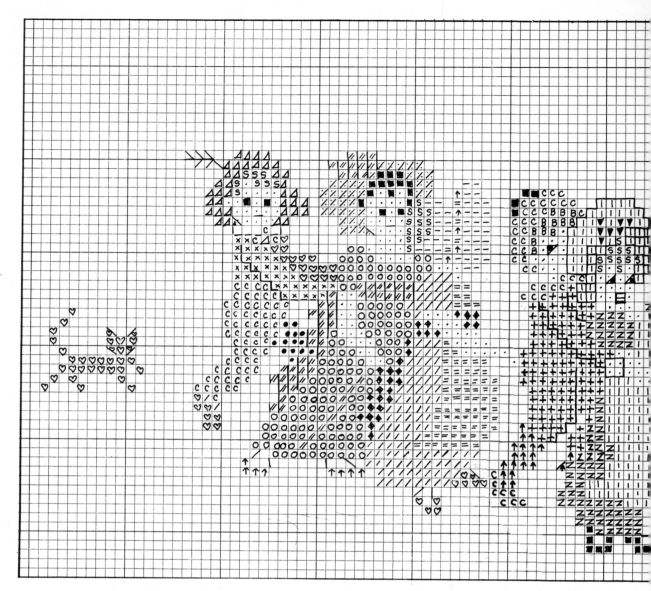

Children on Parade

Size: 55 x 133; centers as marked

DMC #

COLOR CODE:

◪	926	blue green
◪	924	dark blue green
↑	732	dark yellow green; backstitch sash, bow on last girl; pants and sleeve on sixth child
⊞	3013	light yellow green
▼	350	dark coral; backstitch waist, petticoat on first child
◿	352	light coral
⊡	963	flesh pink
⊡	351	coral
◿	644	light beige
∟	642	beige; backstitch umbrella pole
⊟	3045	mustard
■	801	dark brown; backstitch eyes (see note)
⊟	760	light dusty rose; backstitch all flesh details; cross-stitch mouth on fifth child
⊡	3328	medium dusty rose

COLOR CODE:

DMC #

▼ 435   golden brown
▨ 729   medium old gold
Ⓢ 433   medium brown
Ⓞ 677   very light old gold
☒ 676   light old gold
◈ 892   dark geranium
Ⓝ 825   blue; backstitch hat brims on fouth and fifth child
☒ 3024 light taupe gray; backstitch stockings on fourth, seventh and eighth child
◙ 3022 medium taupe gray
Ⓘ   ecru
Ⓩ 519   sky blue; backstitch feather, collar, sleeve on last child
Ⓑ 422   light brown
⊟ 894   light geranium
    680   dark old gold; backstitch pants, collar on third child
    347   red; backstitch hat, feather on third child

NOTE: Work all eyes with one thread of floss only. Where ¾ stitches are indicated, it is necessary to pierce the center of the square of fabric.

19

Girl Singing

Size: 33 x 70; centers as marked

COLOR CODE:

	DMC #	
⊞	3047	light straw
[Y]	676	straw
[O]	718	fuchsia
[S]	434	light brown
■	312	very dark blue
⊟	760	very light red; backstitch hands
⊡	225	flesh pink
▼	552	dark violet; backstitch hat ribbon
⊠	554	lavender
⊜	825	dark blue
⊘	827	light blue
[Z]	841	beige brown
⊡	842	light beige brown

Girl with a Bird

Size: 39 x 64; centers as marked

COLOR CODE:

	DMC #	
⊘	3047	light straw
▣	3046	straw; backstitch hat
[O]	3328	rose
⊡	224	flesh pink; backstitch arms, hands
⊠	647	medium gray
[II]	931	gray blue
[Y]	640	beige
■	414	dark gray
⊠	433	medium brown
⊜	642	light beige

Dolls

Size: 42 x 81; centers as marked

DMC #

☒	898	dark brown
☒	433	brown; backstitch eyes
⊡	818	flesh pink
▣	760	pink; backstitch nose, neck detail
◉	962	light rose; backstitch collar, dress
△	335	dark rose
▣	844	dark gray
℗	743	yellow
▯	754	flesh
▤	813	blue
Ⓢ	420	nut brown
▨	211	lavender
	3348	light green; backstitch flower stems on dress as shown
	415	light gray; backstitch stockings

COLOR CODE:

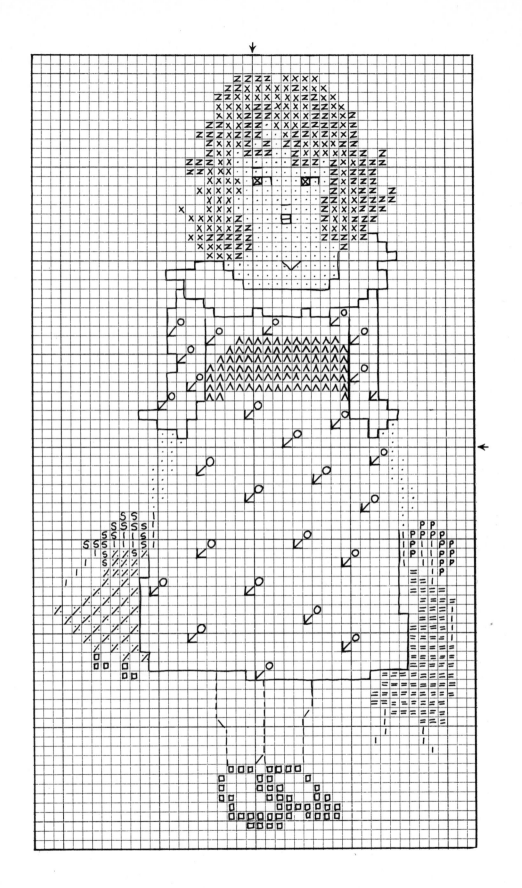

Talisman Rose

Size: 59 x 20; centers as marked

DMC #

COLOR CODE:

- ⊞ 470   green; backstitch stem, thorns
- ☑ 471   light green
- ⊡ 727   light yellow
- ☒ 726   yellow
- ◪ 351   coral; backstitch rose
- ◼ 783   topaz

Fisher Boys Dancing

Size: 66 x 59; centers as marked

DMC #

COLOR CODE:

- Ⓢ 841   light beige brown
- ◉ 921   medium red brown
- ⊠ 434   light brown
- ⊡ 963   pink; backstitch faces, neck
- ◫ 926   gray green
- ☑ 642   dark ecru
- ◪ 838   dark beige brown
- ☑ 535   dark gray; half stitches
- ⊡ 783   topaz
- ☒ 632   dark chocolate brown
- ◭ 826   medium blue
- ▽ 842   very light beige brown
- ⊟ 832   olive green
- ⊟ 3024   taupe
- ☑ 825   dark blue
- ◼ 433   medium brown
- Ⓒ 976   gold brown
-     760   pink; backstitch mouth
-     829   brown; backstitch pants detail
- ⓩ 743   yellow

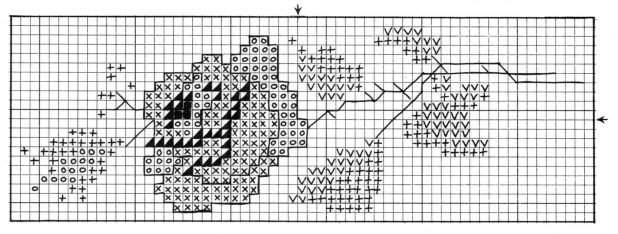

Snowscene

Size: 63 x 81; centers as marked

DMC #

⊞	699	green
☒	321	red
⑤	938	dark brown
⊙	712	ivory
⊡	818	flesh pink
◼	801	brown
⊟	760	pink; backstitch nose
☑	640	beige; backstitch scarves
☑	801	brown; backstitch coat openings

COLOR CODE:

NOTE: Skipped stitches represent snowflakes.

Boy in a Striped Suit

Size: 36 x 78; centers as marked

DMC #

COLOR CODE:

◨ 3371   dark sepia; backstitch hat
⊞ ◼ 433   medium brown; backstitch suit stripes
Ⓢ 975   red brown
▧ 761   pink; backstitch face
⊡ 818   flesh pink
☒ 3045   mustard brown
⊟ 644   medium ecru
▨ 815   cardinal red; backstitch collar

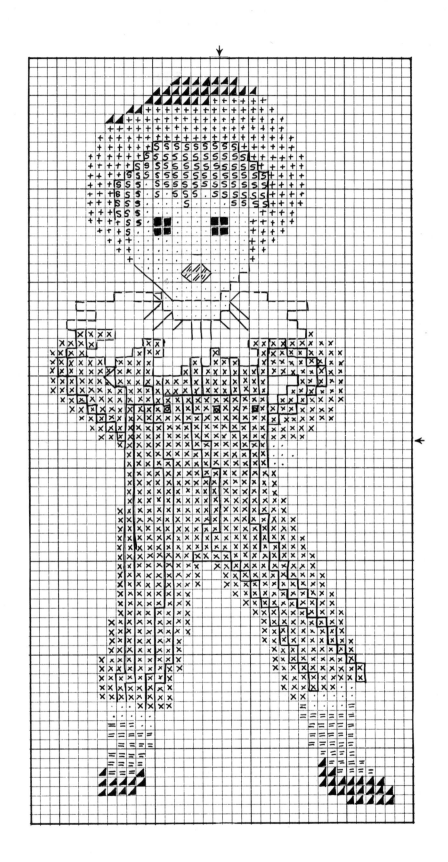

Boy with a Dog

Size: 36 x 71; centers as marked

DMC #

- ☑ 930 antique blue
- ⊞ 840 beige
- Ⓢ 725 yellow
- ⊡ 818 flesh pink
- ◪ ■ 838 dark brown; backstitch brows, umbrella handle, details on dog
- ▣ 760 pink; backstitch face
- ⊙ 922 rust brown
- ☒ 926 green blue
-    924 dark blue green; backstitch coat
- ☑ 920 henna brown
- ⊞ 644 light beige

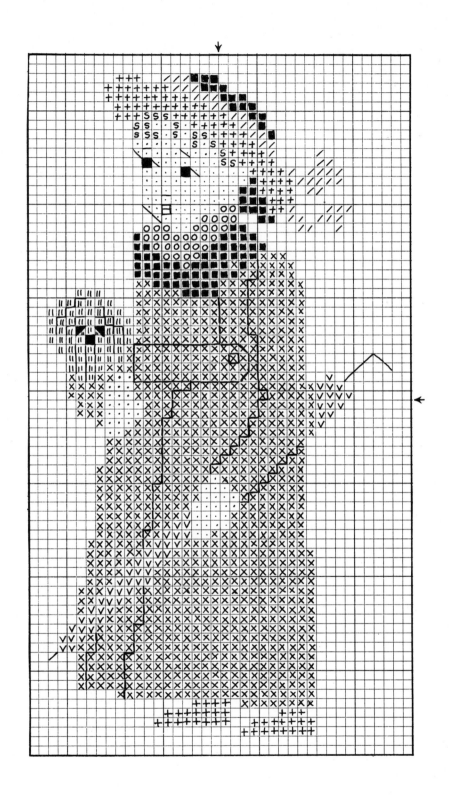

Baby in the Roses

Size: 77 x 65; centers as marked

COLOR CODE:

DMC #

☑	3347	medium green; backstitch details
▣	725	gold
⊟	743	yellow
☒	726	light yellow
◪	351	coral
◼	304	dark rose
Ⓢ	961	medium rose
Ⓒ	309	rose
☑	3326	light rose
☒	963	medium pink; backstitch mouth
⊡	818	pink
☒	869	brown; backstitch eyes
Ⓨ	422	honey
◪	598	aqua; backstitch dress, bonnet
◯	712	cream

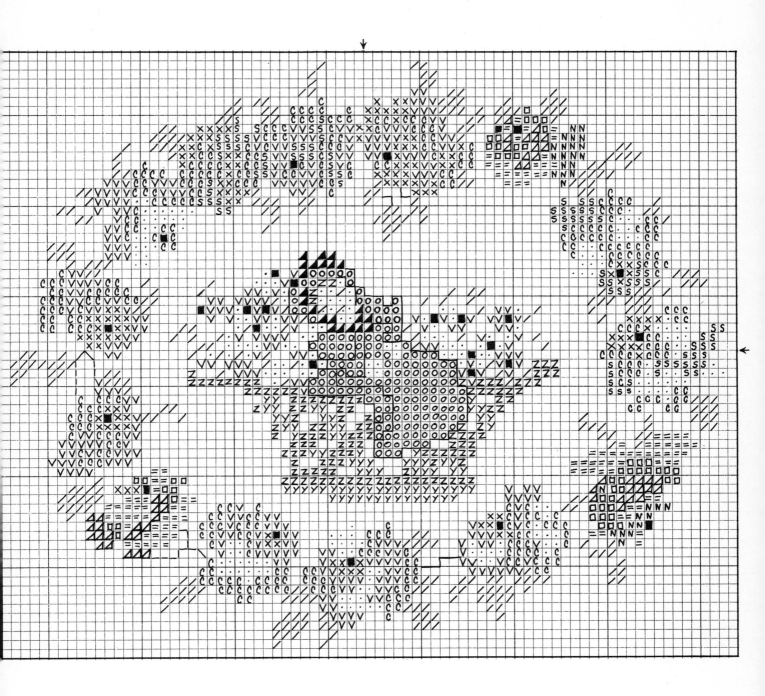

Parasol Girl

Size: 40 x 85; centers as marked

DMC #

COLOR CODE:

☒	760	light rose red; backstitch face, neck
◩	3328	rose red; backstitch parasol, tassel
⊟	712	cream
☒	993	jade green
⑤	433	brown; backstitch umbrella handle
⊡	818	flesh pink
⊞	842	light beige brown
◙	841	beige brown; backstitch mittens
� V	519	sky blue
☒	543	very light beige
	761	very light rose; backstitch face, neck

Rose

Size: 29 x 36; centers as marked

DMC #

COLOR CODE:

⊡	776	medium pink
☒	962	medium rose
◪	309	deep rose
◙	3326	light rose
⊞	937	moss green
◺	469	light moss green; backstitch stem

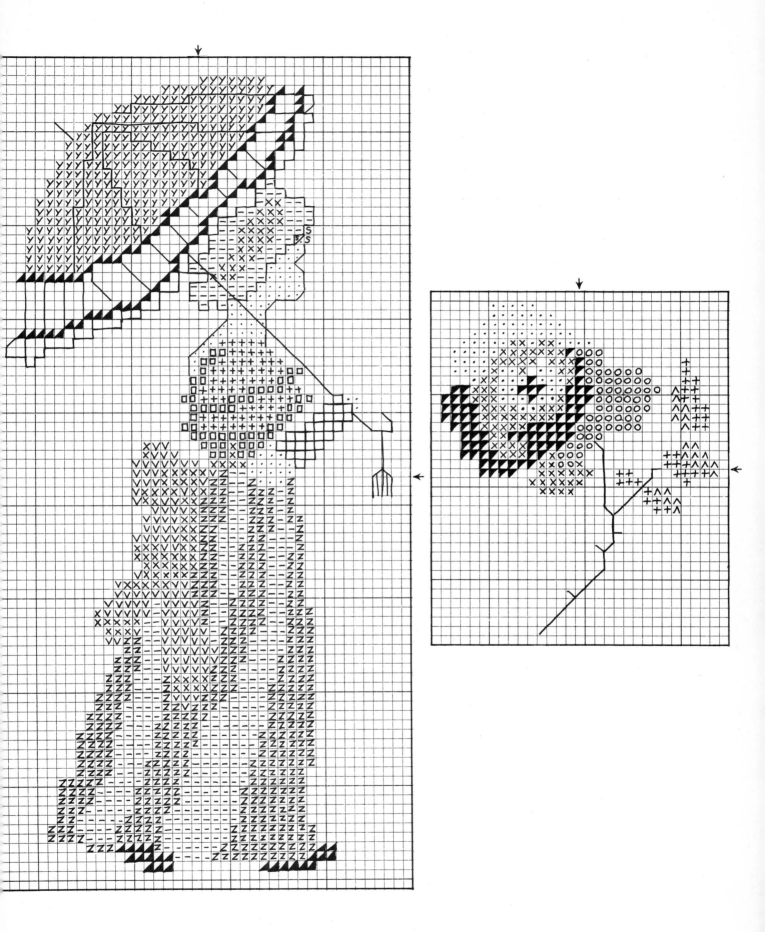

Dorothy and Toto at the Emerald City

Size and centers not given (depends on placement)

COLOR CODE:

DMC #

S 434 brown
Z 801 dark brown
· 963 flesh pink
X 321 red; backstitch collar
O white
Z 436 medium umber
A 780 dark golden yellow
Z 844 very dark gray
II 645 dark gray
⊞ 648 light gray; backstitch stockings
M 743 yellow; backstitch yellow bricks
U 972 orange yellow
Z 702 kelly green
Y 699 dark kelly green
V 704 light kelly green
N 912 medium emerald green; long threads on balloon
⊟ 910 dark emerald green
↓ 518 blue
■ 840 dark beige
□ 842 light beige
Y 955 light emerald green

The Cowardly Lion

Size: 60 x 70; centers as marked

DMC #

COLOR CODE:

⑤	780	dark gold; backstitch details on lion
◢	433	brown
■	310	black
⊠	783	topaz
◯	3072	silver gray
·		white
◿	725	light gold
Ⅲ	645	gray
☒	436	medium brown
⊠	844	very dark gray
⊞	648	very light gray
◙	825	blue
	471	green; backstitch flower stems

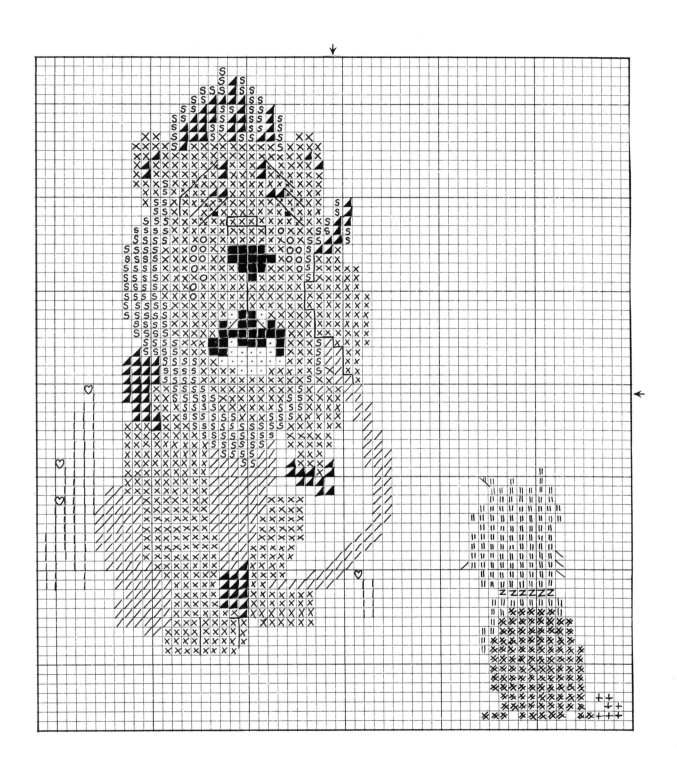

The Tin Woodman

Size: 27 x 59; centers as marked

DMC #

COLOR CODE:
- ⊞ 414   medium gray
- ⊡ 415   light gray
- ☒ 844   dark gray; backstitch details
- ◨ ▣ 310   black

The Scarecrow

Size: 40 x 52; centers as marked

DMC #

COLOR CODE:
- ⧄ 676   light gold
- ☑ 729   medium gold; backstitch bird's perch
- ⊞ 613   light gray beige
- ☒ 826   blue
- ◪ 433   medium brown
- ⊙ 824   dark blue
- ☑ 646   dark gray; backstitch strands and face of scarecrow
- ◨ ▣ 310   black
- ◉ 743   yellow; backstitch beak
- © 347   dark red
- ▲ 433   brown; backstitch mouth

Toto

Size and centers not given (depends on placement)

DMC #

COLOR CODE:
- ▯ 645   dark gray
- ☒ 647   gray
- ▣ 310   black
- ◪ 844   very dark gray
- ⊞ 648   light gray

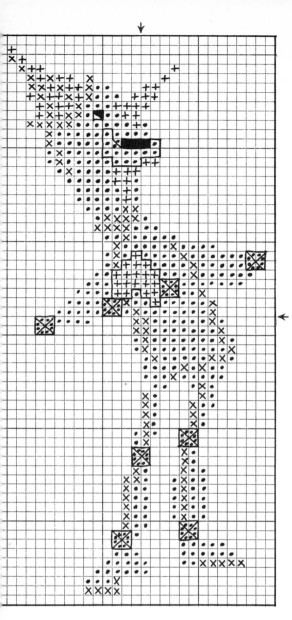
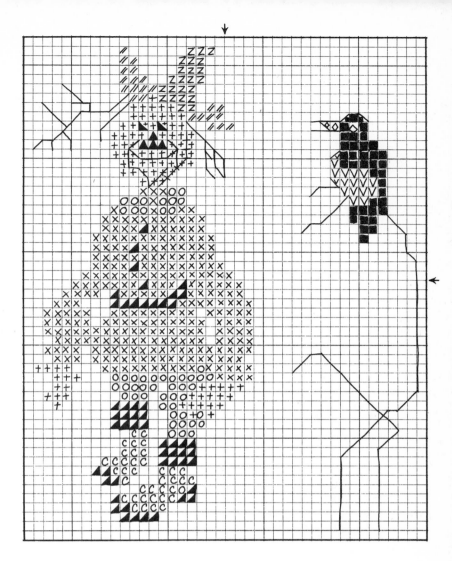
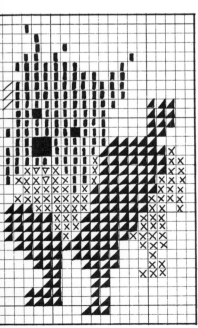
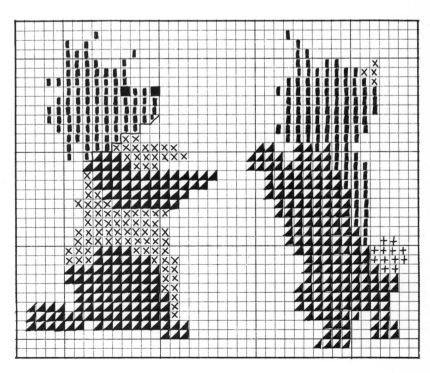

Dorothy and the Silver Shoes

Size: 56 x 53; centers as marked

COLOR CODE:

DMC #

■	310	black; backstitch Toto's nose
⊡	963	flesh pink
Ⓢ ◣	433	dark brown; backstitch eyes
Ⅴ	435	brown
⊠	321	red; backstitch collar
⊿	648	light gray
Ⓨ	645	gray; backstitch around silver shoes
⊞	3072	very light gray; backstitch stockings
◿	844	very dark gray
⊞	648	light gray
Ⅲ	645	dark gray
	760	pink; backstitch mouth, nose

NOTE: If you want to make slippers ruby, as in the movie, instead of silver, as in the book, use DMC #498 ruby red.